Jean-Claude Carrière is a legend in cinema and theatre. He has written the script for award-winning films such as *Diary of a Chambermaid*, *Belle de Jour* and *The Tin Drum*. As a playwright, he worked with Peter Brook for twenty-four years. Their work includes *The Tragedy of Carmen*, apart from *The Mahabharata*.

Aruna Vasudev is known in the world of cinema as the director of several film festivals, including Cinefan, the first festival in India to showcase Asian films, and the publisher of *Cinemaya*, the Asian film quarterly. She has directed and produced several short and documentary films.

BIG BHISHMA IN MADRAS

In Search of the Mahabharata with Peter Brook

Jean-Claude Carrière

Translated from the French by Aruna Vasudev

SPEAKING TIGER

SPEAKING TIGER PUBLISHING PVT. LTD
4381/4, Ansari Road, Daryaganj
New Delhi 110002

First published in French by as *A La Recherche du Mahabharata: Carnets de voyages en Inde avec Peter Brook* in 1997
First published in English as *In Search of the Mahabharata: Notes of Travels in India with Peter Brook 1982-1985*, in 2001

This edition published by Speaking Tiger in hardback in 2018

Original copyright: Jean-Claude Carrière 1997
Translation copyright: Aruna Vasudev 2001

ISBN: 978-93-88326-49-0
eISBN: 978-93-88326-19-3

10 9 8 7 6 5 4 3 2 1

The moral rights of the author have been asserted.

Typeset in Palatino by SÜRYA, New Delhi
Printed at Sanat Printers, Kundli

All rights reserved.
No part of this publication may be reproduced, transmitted,
or stored in a retrieval system, in any form
or by any means, electronic, mechanical,
photocopying, recording or otherwise,
without the prior permission
of the publisher.

This book is sold subject to the condition that it shall not, by
way of trade or otherwise, be lent, resold, hired out,
or otherwise circulated, without the publisher's
prior consent, in any form of binding
or cover other than that in
which it is published.

CONTENTS

Acknowledgements	7
Translator's Note	9
Foreword	11
Arrivals and Departures (1982)	15
The Search Continues (1984)	75
Journey's End—And a Beginning (1985)	99
Afterword	121

ACKNOWLEDGEMENTS

These notes were made between 1982 and 1985 during our first three travels through India in search of the *Mahabharata*. As my original sketches mysteriously disappeared in the course of their travels, I have made new ones for this edition.

All this is thanks to Peter Brook who knows how to make possible the impossible.

TRANSLATOR'S NOTE

When I met Jean-Claude Carrière at his home in Paris, it was to discuss his coming to Delhi where he was going to do a workshop for us, for my Asian film journal *Cinemaya*, on script writing. It was a major event which was to be held at the Cultural Centre of the French embassy which, in those long-ago days, had a small auditorium where we had shown films and held different workshops over a number of years. Jean-Claude Carrière agreeing to come and do a workshop was a huge achievement.

When we met and discussed this in Paris, he presented me with his book *A La Recherche du Mahabharata*. I had not seen the 9-hour play Carrière had written and Peter Brook had presented in France. The film had not yet been made.

I read the book while I was still in Paris and went back to say to Jean-Claude that it MUST be translated into English. He just laughed and said, 'Why don't you do it, Aruna.'

It was quite a challenge but I thought 'why not. It should be read in India and elsewhere by English-speaking people because it is such an inspiringly written account of something most people outside India, do not know about.' And within India it gives such a moving insight into the role of the *Mahabharata* in our lives.

I returned to Delhi a few days after meeting Jean-Claude, and started the translation immediately. I finished it within the next couple of months. When Jean-Claude arrived in Delhi a few months later to conduct the workshop we had planned, he read it and said, 'It reads better in English than in French.'

Incorrigible as I am, my response was, 'Of course. I know English better than you know French!' It got published very quickly and launched by the then Ambassador of France in India, Bernard de Montferrand, at a lovely ceremony at the French embassy.

It was a very happy moment for me and the book did get good reviews and good sales.

Now I am delighted a new edition is being published by Speaking Tiger all these years later. Jean-Claude Carrière had done a number of sketches for the first edition but now, he has done new ones for this edition which give a new life to his story and the story of his travels through India with Peter Brooke, in search of the *Mahabharata*, in a very evocative and appealing manner. Hopefully, it will also lead to the film being shown again.

ARUNA VASUDEV
New Delhi, October 2018

FOREWORD

Jean-Claude Carrière was the main reason I stuck out what turned out to be a life-changing five-year adventure for me.

It was April 1984. I was five months pregnant with my first child, and had been in bed with jaundice for four months. That is how Peter Brook, Jean-Claude, Marie-Hélène and the two designers, Chloe and Pippa, first saw me, at my home in Ahmedabad. Two days earlier I had received a telegram from my friend, the cultural attachè at the French embassy in Delhi, saying that they wanted to see me. I was surprised and presumed it was for some minor role. I didn't know Peter's work but had read news reports of his casting quest in India. Within ten minutes of our meeting, Peter asked me to audition for the role of Draupadi. I was flabbergasted. Draupadi had always been my favourite character, feisty, unyielding, vocal. There was a catch, of course, and that was that the play was in French (I didn't know the language) and that the contract would be for two years. I was about to be a mother, had just started a publishing company with my then husband, and the prospect sounded frightening.

However famous Peter was, I knew that I had to like his work before even considering the offer. In New York a week later I watched his *Carmen*, and was blown away. I told Peter I would audition. I was flown to Paris and made to do an audition at two in the morning at Peter's theatre, the Bouffe du Nord. I was offered the role, three weeks off early rehearsals to have my baby, and that was that.

Moving to France with a tiny baby, setting up home for the first time, not speaking the language, in the midst of the worst winter in years, with frozen piping in my apartment, and a rehearsal space which was an eight-floor walk up, was hard. And I disliked the atmosphere of the rehearsals. Every other actor was a star theatre actor from one country or another. I was a dancer. I was the only Indian and the only one amongst the actors who knew and had read and reread many versions of the *Mahabharata*. I had problems with women being interpreted as shrews. (There are no shrews in the *Mahabharata*, I told Peter, only Shaktis!) I disagreed with the way many scenes were interpreted. And I only had Jean-Claude to turn to, a man in charge, English-speaking, encouraging and understanding of my loneliness and despair.

I learnt French. Began to speak it well, in fact.

I learned to hold my own. I made good friends. I started unpeeling myself like an onion as an actor. I learned to be knowledgeable enough to be able to put up cogent arguments for why I thought certain scenes were wrongly interpreted. Previews started. I found women of all kinds reacting positively to my interpretation of Draupadi. We started touring the world. Then came the English version, then the film. And five years had gone by.

All the performance work I have done since, the work I create to bring about changes in mindsets and attitudes, were born in my experience playing Draupadi to diverse audiences. The confidence I got as a storyteller also comes from there. And through it all Jean-Claude remained a friend to turn to, a shoulder to cry on, and a buddy to celebrate with.

This book has been a fascinating read for me too because it predates my adventures with the troupe. And his squiggles are always a delight, capturing as they do, the prana of the figure he has drawn.

MALLIKA SARABHAI
27 September 2018

Arrivals and Departures
1982

DELHI

We knew the poem, we wanted to see the country. India. We had read the *Mahabharata* at length, Peter in English, Marie-Hélène Estienne and I in French, in Hippolyte Fauche's version. After listening to Philippe Lavastine's long and marvellous accounts; after one year of reading—in Paris, while travelling, everywhere. Another year of reading together, around a table. Comparing versions, eliminating certain digressions, some preliminary accounts ('Yayati', for example, not without regret).

The *Mahabharata* had been, for eight years, our constant companion. I took it with me to Mexico when I worked with Buñuel (Portolés, the Spanish filmmaker). Always one or two volumes in my suitcase, since the whole work is impossible to carry— sixteen times the size of the Bible! I remember a day in New York in 1983, auditioning tenors for *Carmen*. Seated beside Peter in a theatre. At an audition one knows immediately whether a singer is good or not. Then, out of politeness, one listens for another ten minutes. Peter leaned slightly towards me and whispered something about Karna, 'Don't you think that?...' I don't remember exactly what it was about. But he could think only of that. I, too.

And the tenor carried on singing.

In India now, together, familiar with the story, the characters. Capable of discussing them with the Indians, even with the specialists.

But needing India. Needing to see how the *Mahabharata* is still acted, danced, sung, lived. During several preparatory journeys, Marie-Hélène had been in touch with a large number of schools, artists who sang, danced and acted in episodes of the poem. And who, indeed, does not do that? And some who even do nothing but that. We were to see plenty of them.

But above all we needed to see and to hear India. Meet, gather *all* the images. Not to have, for the moment, any idea of the spectacle, of the play. To remain open, curious, a little childlike. Go everywhere.

We had the advantage of knowing nothing. No *a priori*. We were not experts.

September 1982. I find myself in India for the first time.

I arrive in Delhi in the middle of the night. I have an address, that of a cultural attaché who is supposed to look after me for a few hours. I have to take a flight at dawn for Bombay where Peter awaits me.

No money, no loose change to make a phone

call. Nobody at the airport. Pay the taxi in dollars (exchange counter closed).

In the long avenues of Delhi, in the dead of night, my first sight of cows, like pale ghosts.

I arrive in Bombay the next day. A small hotel (we are on a tight budget). The *Bhagavad Gita* in my room, so also the Bible.

I find Peter, Marie-Hélène, our music director Toshi, and Simon, Peter's son. We are to travel together, all five of us.

My first newspaper, my first bizarre news item: a factory owner swears before the judge that he did not throw the workers into the river.

The first night, shots of firing wake us up. The next day Peter inquires at the front desk of the hotel. Gunshots? Are you sure? Peter is sure, so am I. But the boss has heard not the slightest sound of any shooting; nor have any of his employees. When Peter insists the man replies, 'It was the storm.'

Saturday, 21 August

The first day in Bombay. Into the swing of things immediately. Plunging into the chaos of the city, encounters with directors and actors, with Girish Karnad, with Vijaya Mehta. Dancers too. We announce our plans: present the *Mahabharata* on the stage, in French. And why not? First tricky questions. But it is all right, we know the work. It is familiar territory.

In the evening, the popular theatre. Girls dance on the stage, men get up and give them rupees. Like an age-old game of seduction, easy and open, without tourists. A lovely wooden hall.

At night, on foot, in the streets. Vendors sitting in their stalls, surrounded by fruits, dressed in white.

No torpor. On the contrary. A vibrant vitality.

ELEPHANTA
WAITING TO SELL
WATER TO THE TOURISTS

We are told we must not miss Ellora and Ajanta. An obligatory tourist circuit. The plane up to Aurangabad, then chauffeur-driven cars, one day for Ellora, one for Ajanta. But tourism is also a part of travelling. Pointless to deny it.

Images fashioned in stone. Ellora is mixed Hindu and Buddhist. Ajanta only Buddhist. Groups of Japanese on a pilgrimage to these sacred sites. Toshi speaks to them.

Our driver is Muslim and does not hide it. His disdain for Hindu festivities (marriages, processions) which we encounter on the way, and which we want a closer look at. Many stops, which exasperate him.

Ellora, a frieze-like mountain. With the landscape like an ornamental backdrop. Sculpting the earth (the temple of Kailash is entirely cut out of a single piece of rock. But how could anyone know that there was a temple in the mountain?).

A few days in Bombay. Film screenings. The *Mahabharata* in Hindi films adapts itself easily to the modern world: for example, two families of bankers destroy each other. Not for us.

Heat and rain. End of the monsoon. We are leaving for the south. Everyone tells us: 'It is the best season.'

Bombay, Chor Bazaar, an incredible collection of bric-a-brac. It seems that one finds *everything* here.

Everything is carried, or pulled, by men. People, things, everywhere is on the move. It is like a miracle. It feels as if the streets will freeze with the surcharge. But no. A surprising fluidity. The dharma of the masses. The present is sometimes very ancient.

❖

The plane for Bangalore, then another car. And more tourism.

First of all Shravanabelagola, in Karnataka. Twenty-five kilometres away, across the vast plain, one sees the gigantic statue of the Jain saint, Gomateshvara, a very illustrious personality. Every ten or fifteen years he is given a ritual bath; very special ablutions.

A KIND OF DANCING CLOWN IN A VILLAGE (KARNATAKA)

We walk six hundred and nineteen steps up to the top of the hill. Toshi arrives first. The towering stone giant stands in the courtyard of a temple. More than seventeen metres high. The gentle hermit is totally naked. Plants sculpted in stone snake up his legs.

His penis is enormous. I imagine it, from time to time, under the effect of certain astral conjunctions and accompanying prayers, swelling and rising, spraying the audience with semen which impregnates all the women present.

It is time to start inventing Indian myths. The best is that these myths, still very much alive, are open to the imaginings of people faraway.

The next day, inevitably, the temples of Belur and Halebid, also in Karnataka. The usual state of wonder in front of this 'lacework in stone'. Bare feet burn on the stone floor of the courtyard; a puja in Belur; eroticism of the sculpted dancers and, in some places, episodes that we start to recognise. At Halebid, for example, Bhishma on his bed of arrows. And here and there, a little sodomy in between other practices going back to eternity.

And then, Udipi, close to the Indian Ocean, still in Karnataka, for our first visit to a school of dance, the Yakshagana.

Here a tradition going back several centuries has been completely revived and revitalized by a great master. We watch the classes (training starts from the age of six) and, on two successive evenings, performances accompanied by commentaries.

Emotion: suddenly recognising 'our' characters but in the land that gave them birth. Recognising also scenes and episodes, trying to identify the language, the signs. Each dancer here dances the same role all his or her life, until the dancer and the character become indistinguishable one from the other. Arjuna is over sixty, something that does not seem to upset anyone—especially not him!

Costumes and make-up are lighter than in Kathakali. But the need for *transfiguration* is obvious. The dancer, the actor, is someone else. Long discussions on techniques of gestures, of the eyes. They show us their *Mahabharata*. For us to find ours.

30 August

By car to Kerala, towards the south. Headed for Cannanore.

At first we had planned to take two cars for the five of us. In the end one suffices. It is an Indian Ambassador car. In any case, India has only that. Towards the end of the 1940s, a model had been found which was perfectly suited to the country: slow motor, heavy body, very sturdy. A driver always with us (steering wheel on the right, inherited from the British). Two sit in front with the driver, three at the back. Since the seats in the middle are the least comfortable, we change places now and then. Long distances, frequent stops. A carrier on top of the car for the baggage, Toshi's instruments, our shopping. The driver can stay eight days with the clients. In the evenings he disappears to eat and sleep, who knows where. It's a secret.

In the car, time to see, time to reflect. All together and each one on his own.

The eroticism of the *Mahabharata*. As soon as a rishi retreats into the forest to do penance, a stunningly sexy woman emerges from the river to distract him. But for that at least two or three beautiful women would be needed. There is something humid and hot in the poem, something primeval. Almost everything starts with a royal hunt, with a king who falls asleep, dreams of his wife and his sperm escapes. Not to be missed. Ganesha might say: 'It is a good beginning.'

The force of destiny, the strength of desire. One often pitted against the other, alas.

In Cannanore for a few days from where we make short trips.

They say it is in Kerala that the traditions of the *Mahabharata*, at least in the performances, are the most faithfully preserved.

First of all in Kathakali, the dance form best known in the West (several visits to the Kathakali centre, several performances). It is perhaps to a Kathakali performance that Peter saw in London to which we owe our presence in India today. He recollects a particularly striking moment: a strangely dressed creature thrusts his head ferociously into the entrails of another creature and comes up with a red ribbon—the intestines—between his teeth. He wondered what it was all about. Today we know that it was Bhima settling accounts with the terrible Dushasana.

In 1975, an Indian company came to Paris. We went to see their performance and we showed them ours—*Ubu aux Bouffes* (Ubu at the Bouffes Theatre) it was called at that time, then *Ubu Roi* (king), then *Ubu Cocu* (cuckold). Naturally they did not understand a word of French. At the end, we kept them back in the theatre and Peter asked them to tell us in their way, in their language (without make-up or costumes), what they had understood of the play. One of them started, with beautiful hand gestures, 'There was once a powerful king surrounded by courtesans.' He had understood perfectly the idea of a conspiracy against a cruel king. One thing struck them as an obstacle: the fact that an actor could play several characters without—almost—changing his appearance. An impenetrable convention.

In that same period we had started taking some dance lessons from Karuna (Kathakali guru living in Paris, and Peter's brother-in-law). To get used first of all, to bending the knees, the weight on the outside

edge of the feet, the back straight. Learning some hand gestures and movements of the eyes. What the body can express—when one forces it—of another culture and which the mind cannot conceive of![1]

We meet them again. Still amazing. Incredible complexities of appearance—terrifying, melancholy or disdainful, and even burlesque. As if feelings were hidden away, to be expressed only by the eye or a movement of a finger. Sacred dances, bringing alive myths, sometimes the most hallowed ones (the *Gita*). The necessity of sharing at least some elements of a language of sign and gesture. The story told is already familiar to those who watch it unfold. The audience keeps coming back to be reminded of it, or to admire a particular artiste.

A very effective stage design, square, the audience seated on the ground, overshadowed by the living heroes.

A tranquil majesty, sometimes almost clownish (in our eyes). An inexplicable tradition (are not they all?). Here the theatre has a rigorous code. If one takes it, in fact, to be theatre.

And the contemporary perversions: they tell us that certain groups present Kathakali in front of four

---

1. In July 1985, in the courtyard of the Palais Vieux in Avignon, while a play was going on, I was called upon to dance in public with Karuna. I played (but without make-up) Bhima who strangles the wily Kichaka.

or five thousand people, under huge tents, to the raucous music of today. Nothing is spared.

Kerala, home of Theyyam. Another traditional performing art, directly linked to the temple.

Our first encounter with this is in a little temple (name forgotten), by a river. We are allowed to attend a ceremony, the first time for us. Two hundred fervent devotees, incense, prayers, offerings, the Brahmins—young and agile—distributing flower petals to the assembled crowd. One of them, who seems to be about eighteen, has a golden plaque on his forehead.

It is something that has been untouched by time. No tourists, not even Indian. Then comes the head priest, dressed in a strange costume, half-armour, half-flowers. Very odd. Quite astonishing. He carries two silver swords and starts his dance in the middle of the audience, brandishing his arms. Very quickly he seems to go into a trance. But controlled? He charges towards me, raises a sword with both hands, swings it down on my head, stopping two centimetres from my hair.

A sort of 'sacred frenzy'. Words from antiquity come to the lips, words like 'idol-worshippers'. A sense of intoxication, of a contact with something unexpressed, inexpressible. Is it theatre, or not theatre? We stay about two hours. At the end, a moment of silence beside the river.

Three times, and always at night, we are taken to other temples, to see other dances, this time in the open air—once even with elephants.

First of all, the make-up, very slow, very meticulous. The dancer lies still for about two hours. Minute by minute he becomes a god—or at least the vehicle borrowed by the god through which he manifests himself.

Then his costume is put on, very complicated and weighing up to fifty kilos. They do his hair, put a light wooden trellis frame around his waist, sew on some parts of his costume. Each mask is different, sometimes huge, very elaborate and often frightening—except for the monkey-god Hanuman who makes one laugh. An extraordinary creature, red and black, who comes out of the night from who knows where.

Four or five percussionists, one of whom is a singer, accompanies them. The drums keep going; at times the beat grows louder. Faster. And the dancer follows. It seems as if the god must first enter into the character who awaits him: he shivers, jerks, his helpers rush around, torches are handed to him. Then his movements begin, to the rhythm of the music, he spins round and round. His face is hidden, you can see only his black eyes.

This is when, they say, he showers his blessings. When he stops, after twenty to thirty minutes, someone else replaces him. Sometime two or three dance together. 'Dance' is perhaps saying too much. The sheer weight of their costumes cannot allow them to actually dance. It is more like heavy, rhythmic steps punctuated with leaps in the air. Truly extraordinary. Once again it is difficult to call it theatre, a play.

Plenty of fire, plenty of brandishing of arms, flurry of movements. It is a veritable sword dance. Constant violence, terrifying at moments. Here there is no language to understand. The effect is direct. Incantations. This world is brutal and bloody. Patently. The gods know it. Besides, they themselves…

The long, red, nights of Kerala. Everywhere.

One day we pass through Mahé, a former French trading post in India. Strange to see wine and liquor shops lining the road. Is this a hangover of the French presence? This our legacy?

First questions. Do we start with the origins? Keep a part of the myth with, for instance, a narrator?

Or, on the contrary, plunge straightaway into the drama as in a tragedy with, for example, a violent scene—of which there are plenty—between the adult Kauravas and the Pandavas.

The second possibility is perhaps too 'Occidental'. Both dimensions must be kept, even if they are self-contradictory: the narrative, like a meandering river covering several generations with their parallel stories, and the concentrated story, the drama, around the *conflict*.

In any case, the conflict is central. Peter wonders whether the heart of the poem is not just that, a grandiose attempt to define the notion of 'conflict'.

Why do we fight? And for what?

What is there within us that fights?

A mystery-conflict.

Three days of rest (alone with Peter) at Kottakkal on the west coast, in a centre of traditional Ayurvedic medicine. We need to look at things in perspective, to talk.

A pleasant place. And the treatments—potions to drink, vigorous massage with warm coconut oil. Two masseurs, one on either side. They go about it gaily. The effect is very good.

Visit the large garden where they grow medicinal plants used in this traditional system all over India.

An air of magic: they show us, for example, the plant which 'solidifies water', and some which keep the demons at bay. Ready to believe everything (living in another world, another mentality). Over here they make 'helmets of herbs' which one must wear all night long for one week (they are changed every day) and which can cure mental illnesses.

Two successive evenings we are invited to dine with the proprietor in his home opposite the clinic. An immense house crawling with servants. Speciality: the large dining room is on four levels, according to the degree of importance of the invitees. Three or four steps between each level. We are on the top level, with the owner. Men only.

The slaves bring us thalis, plates, supervised by a very superior person, an elderly man with white hair, wearing a lungi, whom we immediately call the slave master. Once again it is a journey into the past. It could easily be a patrician home in ancient Rome, with clients received according to their status and, undoubtedly, huddled somewhere at the back of the house, the poor.

As always in India, meals taken rapidly, in silence. In less than ten minutes it is over. The owners eat, naturally, with their fingers, heads bowed, mixing vegetables and sauces with rice placed in the centre of the plate. Rare are the moments when food appears to be a pleasure worthy of appreciation. A balanced

Big Bhishma in Madras

meal, vegetarian, consisting of local, regional products has been found once and for all, and it never varies. In the whole of the south we eat more or less the same thing, twice a day. A foreigner enjoys it the first time, perhaps even the second. The third time, he starts to find it boring. At the end of one week, he forgets that he is eating. For a change, we stop from time to time in a village to have an onion omelette cooked on a charcoal fire out in the open. Always delicious. When we get to a big city (Madras, Calcutta), we will go to a restaurant in a grand hotel to regale ourselves with chicken and lamb and watch the dancers undulating.

ALL VEGETAL
KERALA

JCC

In Kottakkal, evening; end of the day. Peter goes for a walk alone among the palm trees across the rice fields. He comes back marvelling at the peace, the silence, the solitude, at the stone houses of Kerala, the singing of the insects at twilight, the little paths through the already tall rice fields.

The last day, just before leaving, he is told that the rice fields are full of particularly dangerous snakes. Hence the solitude and the peace!

By car to Trichur. Long discussions about energy, its rise and fall. A question that has always fascinated Peter—understandably. What is it that creates the energy, the intensity that one senses at times in the theatre? Only on certain evenings, at certain moments? Can it be measured *scientifically*? Will that ever be possible? When human energy is at its peak does it become one with another which could be called cosmic?

How can one find it? How can one hold on to it?

Three hours of discussion, on a slow drive going from one river to another, through the green hills of Kerala.

Kerala is a delight. Very hot, humid, tropical. Forests of coconut palms. Many meetings with dancers, actors, musicians. Improvisations, unexpected concerts. An insatiable pleasure in acting, singing.

Houses built of stone, solid, cool. We stay in a hotel by the sea. Quite pleasant but broken down. The roof of the dining room has completely collapsed. I meet a young woman from Delhi who is here alone to work. She is designing textiles.

Must not try to grasp everything, understand everything. Let things flow, at first, without trying to plumb their depths. A quick, superficial first impression is perhaps the best.

We defer all analysis, all categoric judgement. Peter often speaks, even while working, of a 'naive look'. One of our strengths: our ignorance.

We are very active, always ready to take off. Impossible to keep track of everything. In Trivandrum, a festival of martial arts is rather disappointing. Called Kalaripayattu. Lances, swords, bare hands. But the heroes tend to be on the plump side. Gestures uncertain. Indians flatter themselves on having invented these martial techniques, which were Buddhist in the beginning because the use of weapons was forbidden. Toshi turns up his nose.

Nevertheless we have to include them. There are numerous battle scenes and fights in the poem. What is one to do?

We find, and admire, a belt made of sharp steel nearly three metres long, which is tied around the waist and which, properly used, can cut off a head. But of course, say the Buddhists, it is not a weapon, it is a belt.

Peter decides we should have this in the play. It is very dangerous, they warn us. It doesn't matter. Alain (Maratrat) will take charge of it.

3 September

We leave for Madurai by car. It takes a whole day, with a stop at Palani. We go from one end of the continent to the other, and from Kerala to Tamil Nadu (a different culture, a different writing on the signposts and hoardings).

A great shock: the Meenakshi temple at Madurai. We had been warned but all the same...The temple possesses and swallows up the city. Immediately plunged into the past; it is Babylon dreamt up by Cecil B. deMille and directed by an Indian. It is totally, incredibly, full of life. The hall of a thousand columns, the dark statues in every corner, vendors selling everything, the sacred elephant, groups of pilgrims from all over India, specially dressed and

MADURAÏ

TAMIL NADU

made up, like dandified Shivas. The crowd is not too noisy. Some of them carry sackfuls of coconuts on their heads. Some have come like this on foot, covering hundreds of kilometres. The atmosphere is difficult to grasp, even more difficult to describe. Like entering into a dream. Must come back. How to transpose even a whiff of this to the Bouffes du Nord (a theatre in Paris).

A thought for St Jean of the Cross: 'We do not travel to see, but to not see.'

Here, how can one *not* see? At least for a moment.

The elderly, those who have sought renunciation, those who have nothing, seem to compete with each other in the oddness of their appearance. We stand out in the crowd, almost demanding to be noticed. Many come to this temple to ask for a husband or a wife. The offerings are made accordingly. The smell of vegetation is pervasive. All the odours of the vegetal world.

Baroque, tumultuous, chaotic, a torrent, the stuff of fantasy, strange, surcharged: no adjective suffices. We have not seen anything like it anywhere in the world.

❖

And what if, behind this appearance of massive disorder, of this babel of divergent sounds, lay hidden a clandestine dream of unity?

We stop for a few days in Tamil Nadu, in Tiruchirapally (again the feeling of having gone into another time zone), in Thanur, from Kumbakonam to Chidambaram, where we find again the dancers of stone.

Here there is a sensation of being truly in India. In any case, of being *somewhere*.

On to Pondicherry where of course we find France, at least in the names of the streets and restaurants. It's a little Palavas-les-Flots (a small seaside resort in the south of France). Not disagreeable, but, oh well...I stay away from the Mother's ashram.

In the evening we take off for a village. In the car again; it's becoming exhausting, never sleeping before three o'clock in the morning to get up at six without having really slept.

The *Mahabharata* in one of the Terokutu traditions. Superb. In the village square, with strings and pieces of wood, something very poor, very dusty, but with an overpowering vitality. Costumes, nondescript and torn, makeshift weapons and yet, the work breathes through it all. Since we are fairly familiar with the scenes, we begin to feel very close to the peasants present. We laugh at the same points. We sense the same fears.

Dogs and children are asleep. It is night above the tall trees. Feeble lights. Arjuna and Karna challenging each other under the moonlight.

Passing through a street in Pondicherry our driver points to a building and tells us:

'Very good post office.'

A walk in the evening with Toshi. Dozens of children surround us asking him where he comes from. He replies, 'From Japan.' My turn. I also reply that I am Japanese. It is accepted without question. Nationalities, physical differences, all disappear.

Later, one of the children asks me to send him a postcard of the Eiffel Tower. He does not even dream that he could one day leave here, go to Paris. He will never move out of this place, he knows that. But at least the Eiffel Tower can come to him in the form of a postcard.

We are the strangers who pass in the night. We come, we stop and we leave. They stay. They remain where they are.

In a courtyard at the back, in the middle of piles of garbage, an old bicycle has been thrown away. Everything that could be reused, has been removed. All that remains is a carcass, rusty, worn away.

On a pedal an inscription is still visible: 'Life is just a dream.'

Some of the elements of the *mise en scéne*: When Arjuna goes into the mountains, the Himalayas, to do penance to ask Shiva for the boon of a fatal weapon, he is sometimes shown climbing a very tall pole at least ten or twelve metres high. From on top, wearing a simple loincloth, he speaks to God.

Elsewhere, in the last battle, the one in which Bhima breaks Duryodhana's thigh with a single blow, the two actors start the fight (using clubs) in a temple outside the village. Followed by an increasingly large crowd, they move towards the village, still carrying on their fight. In the central square lies an enormous statue of Duryodhana, fifteen metres long. The two combatants fight on around the clay figure until finally, Bhima breaks the thigh of the statue.

Almost everywhere—in Karnataka, in Kerala, in Tamil Nadu—the actors are behind a simple, cotton curtain, held by two assistants. When all is ready, the assistants lift the curtain and the actors appear.[2]

2. Peter used this twice, with certain modifications—for the appearance, and then the disappearance, of Krishna.

In some places, under a tent, many days are spent making a serpent of flowers. The tent is huge, about sixty square metres, like a gigantic mandala. On the day of the festival, the dancer first dances on the serpent, then rolls frenetically on the petals, destroying the patient masterpiece in a matter of moments.

That is how it is.

Madras. A great centre of music, the capital of Tamil Nadu. A good hotel, at last, and a few days of rest, of relaxation. Fatigue seems to have become our permanent companion.

Several concerts, with Toshi as our guide. He has worked many months in India, especially in Calcutta (his favourite city) where he even has students. He studied the songs of Tagore which have some relation to the *Mahabharata*. To sing them one day? Perhaps. He also plays with Indian musicians; he has a great ability to adapt himself.

We go and visit a very famous flautist (I forget his name) who plays for over an hour; to a temple to hear the chanting of the Brahmins, and to many public concerts. Sometimes we only stay twenty minutes. Arriving late or leaving before the end—no one is bothered. The audience does not seem particularly attentive (or so it appears); people talk, eat, some fall asleep.

And then, a visit to the centre of Bharata Natyam, the most famous dance of India. A big park with bungalows around a theatre. The director of the centre is Rukmini Devi, the great reformer of Bharata Natyam in the twentieth century. Over here one rarely describes a young woman as beautiful. She is 'pretty', 'nice-looking', 'attractive', but very rarely 'beautiful'. It seems that beauty is a quality reserved for women above fifty, a quality that is acquired. Often, when we were to meet a woman who was director of such and such an organisation, we would ask 'What is she like?', and we would be told 'She is beautiful.'

Before meeting Rukmini Arundale, who had agreed to receive us, I asked a man who knew her, 'What is she like?'

'She is very beautiful,' he answered.

And it is true. She is over eighty and does nothing to hide her age. She walks slowly, leaning on a cane. Dressed in white and light beige. Her long silvery hair hangs down to her waist. When she enters the room where we are waiting for her, it is as if a light had entered.

We watch many rehearsals and many dance classes. Groups of young girls who work hard together. It seems as if the dancer never wants to lose touch with the earth. Contrary to our classical ballet which seems always to be poised for a flight—an ephemeral flight, repeatedly begun—here the young women dancers return constantly to the earth, beating down hard with their feet, calling upon it to bear witness, drawing energy from it.

This earth which is created as it is destroyed by the dancer in the course of the dance (how can I express it?). Dance of the world whose secrets are constantly sought to be discovered. A Western ballerina dances with the air, always ready to take flight; a dancer here affirms her oneness with the earth which gave her birth. Her body, firmly planted, launches into a thousand movements, sinuous as a plant, like an extraordinary tree, full of flowers, speaking a secret language. The body is divided into three undulating parts in the form of an 'S'. Strictly no straight line.

This dance is called 'graceful', or 'charming'; superficial terms which hide a profound vitality, sexual energy and a certain smiling violence, a pronounced taste for the enigmatic. Even without understanding the meaning of the movements, the poses and postures, I can watch for hours the dancers who come one after the other, here and there (they are everywhere). I am almost hypnotised in the end. Peter is much less sensitive to this. He finds it instead somewhat 'kitsch'.

One evening in Madras, on an Italian-style stage, we see the *Mahabharata* presented in less than two hours. Expeditiously rendered. Really kitsch, ultra-fast and truly bad. Bhishma is a fat man, pot-bellied and often out of breath. Painted backdrops and little fireworks. Local travesty of Western theatre. Poor operetta, to be quickly forgotten.

Visit to Mahabalipuram; temples by the sea where the Pandavas are celebrated. We return to them as to old friends: the little Draupadi temple, that of Bhima and the big rock where Arjuna (but we're not sure if it was really him) did penance, his long and hard penance on the rock. All the while, a big cat gazed mockingly at him.

First meeting with a saint.

In the countryside, in a temple a few hours from Madras. A dense crowd, as always in such cases, but quite calm. We wait to see him.

Shankaracharya is a one-in-three saint. Since this monastic order (or this brotherhood, this tradition in the heart of Hinduism) was founded, this is how they have been called. They are always three, belonging to different generations—an old man, a mature man and a young man who prepares himself for the succession.

The aged Shankaracharya is a true saint.

BIG BHISHMA IN MADRAS

Apparently a revered person in the history of Hinduism. Perhaps the most venerated in the twentieth century. But now one cannot see him. He does not move out of Kanchipuram, the seat of the order or deviate from his vow of silence. He has not spoken a word for many years.

Around five o'clock in the afternoon, the mature Shankar, a man full of smiles, with a round face and an alert look, receives us on a terrace out in the open. The young Shankar is seated nearby. He listens and looks, without speaking.

A few words are spoken in English, then a translator becomes indispensable.

I ask some questions of the saint (red robe, bare arms, the marks of Vishnu on his forehead, a small topknot and a thin stick of bamboo in his hand). I ask him the reason for Yudhisthira's reticence—whom he considers the central hero of the *Mahabharata* which he calls the Dharmaraj (Dharma-king). Why does he agree to lose his kingdom in the game of dice (a question debated at length among us)? Why this long exile? Why this consistent refusal to fight, to reclaim, if necessary by force, that which is his own by right?

Why, during the battle itself, these perpetual hesitations, these repeated retreats, which sometimes appear like cowardice?

Shankaracharya replies with a big laugh: 'Because

otherwise Arjuna and Bhima would have ended the war too quickly!'

I speak to him also of Krishna, his questionable ruses. I say to him: 'How is it that Krishna, who is a god descended on earth to bring succour in a period of crisis and threats, appears at moments troubled, indecisive? How is it that being himself a god, he does not know what is coming, who is taken unawares, shows surprise and disquiet? Is he really a god, or simply a man?'[3]

Once again the saint laughs full-throatedly and replies: 'That is really a human question!'

Laughter all around.

On a parapet, behind the saint, are seated four young Germans. Blonde hair, blue eyes. They are dressed in white and listen respectfully, immobile. Four angels come from the West, almost translucid against the setting sun.

Calcutta. Meeting with Satyajit Ray. He comes to fetch us from the hotel. We see him from afar: very tall, very handsome, towering above the crowd. Speaks excellent English—remarks Peter.

---

3. Krishna, according to Hindu tradition, is the eighth avatar of Lord Vishnu, the Preserver, who holds the world together.

After lunch he takes us home. A large apartment, somewhat sombre, in a great grey building. Musical instruments. Long conversation about the *Mahabharata*. He had also thought of adapting it for the cinema, for television. But it meant doing it in English, and he did not want that. 'Can you imagine Kirk Douglas as Arjuna?' He is much more positive about our project. The advantage, according to him, of not being Indian. Distanced from it, greater freedom. The famous remote look. He is encouraging. Says he is ready to help us, recommends certain musicians. At the moment he is working with children, something he feels passionately about. And he is selecting music for films other than his own.

We talk of *The Cherry Orchard*, which we have just done, and the connection we found with *The Music Room*. He agrees. We talk a lot about that film. I tell him that the shot of the shimmering chandelier reflected in the glass of wine (presaging the fatal drowning, later on) is to me by far one of the most beautiful in the history of cinema. He thanks me with a smile. Very elegant, very courteous, master of himself.[4]

---

4. We would see him many more times. In Calcutta in 1989, I even watched the first screening of *Branches of the Tree* sitting beside him. For me it is among the three or four best of Ray's films.

Still in Calcutta. We hold a press conference on 13 September. The cultural attaché's name is Jean Racine. Then we spend a whole day, Peter and I, with one of Mother Teresa's nuns. We follow her everywhere. A young Indian, she must be under thirty, dressed in white and blue. Her mission is to go every morning to the overcrowded pavements of the city and collect those without hope, to help them die in dignity.

Her authority is impressive. She finds a man dying and immediately calls some men to help her carry him away. Nobody refuses her. She beckons a rickshaw man with an imperious gesture. The man obeys her, knowing full well he will not be paid.

No room for sentimentality. We help place the dying man in the rickshaw. A ravaged old man, on the threshold of death. A man who has nothing. The young nun directs the operation with very few words. She seems to know exactly what she has to do. No sentimentality, no pity. Very matter-of-fact.

Another time we find ourselves with her in a small train, then at a station. Behind the station, thrown on a heap of garbage, two corpses, barely covered. We look at them for a moment.

We are on our way to the famous 'dying room', filmed by Louis Malle in *Calcutta* in 1968, not without creating a scandal. Nothing seems to have changed. The 'poorest of the poor' are there, dying in silence. There is nothing more to be done for them. They generally die of dysentery. They are taken care of, eased into death. A process often held against Mother Teresa. But what else can be done? From the Christian point of view this life is not the true one. Important to die well; real life is elsewhere. Even for the Hindus?

We give some money and all the medicines we still have with us.

A meeting in his house, a little way outside the city, with Professor P. Lal who is completing a translation of the *Mahabharata* into English verse. He has been working on it for twenty years, publishing his huge work in a series of elegant volumes. One of those rare men (along with the Frenchman Hippolyte Fauche in the nineteenth century who died without having accomplished his task. It was taken up by another Sanskritist, who died also before completing it) who set out to do a complete translation. It is like spending one's whole life with a single book.

An elegant, handsome man, sixty-five years old. Clearly knows the book perfectly. Very interested by our project, he places himself at our disposal. (We meet him several times.)

He believes it possible to adapt the *whole* work for the theatre.

He is coming to Paris. Soon.

CALCUTTA LITTERARY COCKTAIL

At least five or six performances in Calcutta, especially (outside the city) by a young theatre group which presents contemporary Bengali plays with a certain energy. We are removed from all vestiges of tradition: no make-up, no costumes. The audience sits all around the room which has nothing of the theatre about it. We understand none of the words but the vibrations are good. No costumes, no 'lighting'. An impression, at moments, of improvisation. Good teamwork. And today's themes.

Some beautiful women in the audience. They sometimes look boldly at us, eyeing us provocatively with an expression that in the West would be taken as an invitation. But that is not the case. Here one makes love only with the eyes. When we leave at the end, the young woman who, a few minutes earlier had been staring at us, turns and leaves with her friends, without once looking back. Something had transpired, but what?

We listen to the singers, the musicians. It is unending. Watch a narrator following a special ritual. He has to kneel on one knee. He has a single accessory, an object which resembles a sort of paddle. In his hands this object becomes all sorts of things: a club, a bow, a lance, a musical instrument, a woman, a tree, a horse.

Three musicians accompany him, seated behind him. He tells the whole story of the *Mahabharata* (playing the different roles, singing sometimes) in eighteen evenings—eighteen here is a sacred number (the *Bhagavad Gita* has eighteen chapters, for example).

We watch him do an episode from the battle, the death of Drona.

Calcutta, 'City of Compassion'. That is how its inhabitants like to call it. They remember how during the Bangladesh war the city of Calcutta, already overpopulated, nevertheless took in millions of refugees and gave them shelter.

Smell of fresh blood in the early morning, in the Kali temple on the bank of the Ganges. That is where they slaughter the goats. A sombre atmosphere, almost sinister. We look in vain for what we call 'sacred'. In the practice of religion are found poverty, harshness, darkness. And a rapacious greed for money.

After a futile attempt at a modest hotel (our budget put palaces out of our reach), we settled down in the Bengal Chambers, a sort of British-style Indian pension with a common dining table, vast rooms, fans, an Indian lady-proprietor with, naturally, a British manner. Very special. A hybrid place, not without a certain charm and for us, affordable. Peter adores it: an England in disguise, a British masquerade.

One evening, at the home of the Dagar brothers: Indian singing.

Here, among all the instruments of music, the human voice reigns supreme. And one understands why. Nothing left to say, after such singing. To hear it is enough. It is the entire body that listens.

It has been, it still is, very difficult enough to enter into the *Mahabharata*. But how do we get out of it?

What we understand more and more clearly is that the many different levels in the work—multiple, complex, moving from farce (Bhima disguised as a woman in order to choke the life out of Kichaka) to the highest spiritual summit of the *Gita*—are levels that can be found in Indian society, in the Indian mentality. This complexity is all around us. In a society of supposedly sharp distinctions, divided strictly even by caste, it is often the ambiguity which strikes us. Feelings are not always what we think they are. Seriousness, dignity, charm, humour—all present at the same time. With what appears, at least to us, an element of strangeness.

What binds all this together is indisputably a vitality. That is what strikes us most strongly. An incredible energy, everywhere. Unexpected, of course: it is the opposite of the usual image of India.

Still in Calcutta.

We meet a group of Bengali ethnologists who work in India itself. Some have come back from three or four years of study in a village in Rajasthan (different language, different culture). They have just published an inventory they have made (they show it to us) of the stories they collected in this one village. More than seventeen thousand.

Told of our desire to go to Orissa and Bihar to look for the survivors of the *Mahabharata* among the tribal people (in India there are at least fifty million), two anthropologists decide to join us. They are very interested. In India, they say, it is not necessary to go anywhere else. One can find here itself all the eras of history, all the epochs.

We leave (a Land Rover and an Ambassador).

I get into the Ambassador with one of the anthropologists and some of our stuff. Peter, Toshi, Marie-Hélène and Simon in the Land Rover (more chic).

Plenty of zigzags and wrong turnings on the way. Pass through Purulia. As night falls we arrive in the village of Chau. Our car is the first to arrive. No sign of Peter's. While the anthropologist, who speaks a bit of the language, goes off to try and get some news, I sit in front of the house which belongs to the chief, a short, stocky man, very dark and wearing a lungi, strongly resembling an Australian aborigine.

He offers me some water, which I refuse although I am dying of thirst (the bottles of soda water are in the other car), then something to eat: potatoes in a reddish sauce, atrociously spiced. I eat one or two out of politeness. Then I make signs to indicate I am tired, that I would like to lie down and rest while waiting for the others.

Fine. He has a bed brought out into the open, that is to say a wooden frame with interlaced ropes, and tells me to lie down while he carries on with his evening chores. It must be seven or eight o'clock. Before going he tells one of his daughters, dark like him, to keep an eye on me.

She must be twelve or thirteen. While I lie on the ropes, she sits silently, gracefully, near me. I close my eyes. A moment later I feel the little girl's hand very lightly touching my shoulder. I open my eyes: she has brought me a cushion to place under my head. I do so, and close my eyes again. Another moment, another light touch. I reopen my eyes. Without any words, knowing they would be incomprehensible to me, she makes me understand with signs that I am lying partly under a tree on which there are insects, or caterpillars, which could fall on me and sting me.

I get up. With her help I move the bed a little further away and lie down again. She again sits down in silence near me, fanning me with a small fan made of peacock feathers. Above us is the sky, the night. Closing my eyes I have the impression that my sleep is protected by a little girl come from far away, from prehistory, at once younger and much older than me.

I have hardly fallen asleep. The second car arrives and the evening—which lasts the whole night—gets going. First a reception in the courtyard of the chief's house, a courtyard which must measure around thirty square metres. He has grasped that Peter is the head of our delegation. He makes Peter sit opposite him and asks first—through one and at times, two interpreters (the anthropologists): 'Where are you from?'

This question is always primordial. It is translated into English as either 'Where from?', or 'Native place?' Peter replies, with great seriousness, 'London.'

Peter, therefore, is from London. The chief, who hasn't the slightest idea where London is to be found, nods satisfied, and asks the second question: 'Do you have a house in London?'

The phrase is translated for Peter who, still very serious, replies, 'Yes.'

The chief again nods his head. Good. Here is a man who has a house in London. Then comes the third question, as important as the first two: 'How many cows in your house in London?'

Peter smiles, tries to answer. The explanations go on.

During this time a feast is being made ready, and a performance. Very beautiful images, very strong, the strongest since the Theyyam in Kerala.

Here also the actors, back from the fields, with the night all around us, allow themselves to be made up for the roles they are to play. They lie down on their backs and close their eyes; two, three or four hours pass by as the others work in silence around them. Little by little, as in Theyyam, in the hands of his friends, of his neighbours, the peasant becomes a god. Or at least a sacred character. The manners of the others towards him become respectful. As if he has been invested with a new power, which the make-up symbolises. Metamorphosis.

When all is ready around eleven at night, in the village square the feast begins. It lasts the whole night. Everyone is there, even the children who at some point fall asleep. Songs and dances with drums. Scenes we recognise: Arjuna in the mountains fighting in vain with the hunter who was no other than Shiva and who would give him the supreme weapon—which he would never use; then a moment from the *Gita*, the beginning; and Bhima's fight with the terrible Rakshasa in the forest. Very beautiful, very strong, full of sound and fury.

Also the death of Abhimanyu, that marvellous

adolescent, son of Arjuna who in his mother's womb, learnt how to break Drona's discus-like formation of war (*Chakravyahu*). Actually, he heard how to enter into the *Chakravyahu* but not how to get out of it because his mother fell asleep while Arjuna was telling the story.

The death of youth in the war (a war for which it had clamoured). 'These heroes have killed a child'.

At times when a character moves while speaking, especially when he is enraged, a drummer follows closely behind him, like a second voice mute, yet articulate, a striking shadow.

We drink it all in avidly. The Bengali anthropologists take notes. Toshi records the rhythms.

It goes on almost until dawn.

In other Chau villages, dancers use masks, painted on a white background. We take one back for the actor who will play Ganesha, the scribe with the elephant head, patron of artists—and of thieves.

Another place the next morning, a well-known centre we have heard about. A performance organised for us, and paid for by us. But everything is different. A French ballet master passed through here towards the end of the eighteenth century. Something of him still remains in the style, in the rhythms. It is as if they are dancing a minuet, without any sense of conviction, vapidly. (Western dance, English rather than French, only became known at the beginning of the twentieth century.)

In the city now, where a famous guru runs a dance institute. But the guru is absent. Could we still visit the school? We ask the administrator sitting at a desk on a raised platform in the centre of the room. All around him an incredible pile of documents and files thick with dust.

He asks for a translation. Then he thinks about it. Is he authorised to allow us to enter? The effort of thinking shows on his face. He asks a question which is translated for us. We try to answer it. He thinks again. And again. And again. This goes on for more than an hour. The man remains silent for a long while, raises his eyes, asks some more questions. Let us enter the dance school? No. Finally he says no. And we leave.

A palatial building, whitish, pitted by rain, and mysteriously closed.

From time to time, for an hour or two, below a temple, or in the shade of a tree, we sit and read the *Gita*, slowly, with stops and comments.

Return via Benaras, the inevitable stopover, and via Agra where, as the sun sets, we gaze at the dazzling unity of the Taj Mahal. End of exuberance, here is Islam. A perfect work would combine the Taj and the temple of Madurai. But that would be inconceivable.

The visit to Benaras: classic emotion, more or less guaranteed. But everything depends on the order of the voyage. Where one begins, where one stops.

To die in Benaras: the promise, or almost, of *nirvana*. In the streets, a marriage. The bride and groom are decked out like princes. Installed in a sort of horse carriage but pulled by men who carry on their heads, each one of them, a sort of *lighted* neon tubelight. These are actually linked by thick, twisted electric wires to a small generator which follows the procession.

Let each one carry his own light. That is the way it should be.

We have several times slept in the most improbable places. Arrivals in the middle of the night. Nobody, nothing to drink, throats on fire. We were grateful if at times, we found a warm Pepsi-Cola. On two or three occasions I shared a room with Toshi. Bugs, one time, which had to be killed. Noises. Almost all over India a faint, cloying smell of shit.

BIHAR JCC
ON THE ROAD

In Delhi, the circle is complete. Physical exhaustion. The shaded charm of the Imperial Hotel. Even a swimming pool.

We stay four very full days. Lots of meetings, films, visits, parties. Finally, even a little shopping. I write a few bits of scenes, I read, I talk. What sort of adventure is it that have we embarked upon?

The tenacious presence of the *Mahabharata*. It is everywhere, in all forms, even in the piles of comic books (in Hindi and in English). It is perhaps the only really common point between different cultures and languages. Very well known, even among the tribals. More than the gods, more than the laws.

A subcontinent identified by a book. The greatest poem in the world. The most complete? A phrase, arrogant in its way, in the middle of the poem goes: 'All that is in the *Mahabharata* exists in the world. What is not in it, does not exist.'

No point then, in looking anywhere else.

The extreme ambition of the work. The physical effects that it implies (to be seen).

Does the complexity of India correspond to the complexity of the poem? And vice versa? Here nothing is simple, but it can all be analysed. The philosophy does not forbid any tunnel, any jungle. To go even towards darkness (necessary). Contradictions even in our own reactions. It could be compressed into one sentence, 'But what horror, what abasement, never seen such filth.... What marvels!'

The *Mahabharata*: it is also a mixture of emotions; of disquiet, with no sign of light; of shocks, of precise and sometimes cynical descriptions—like a prodigiously ambitious pattern that a genius of a poet (or was it several poets?) attempted to apply to the world, the world that he knew, the India of antiquity.

Make of India of the past, the world of today. But how? In juxtaposing scenes of different colours. Or introducing different colours in the same scenes? And how not to abandon the *action* on the way? Is it possible?

In Kerala today, children are still given names from the poem. Avoiding those which bode ill, like Karna, a bastard rejected by his mother although the son of the Sun. Superb warrior with a huge heart, but so uneasy in the shadows.

The plane leaves Delhi for Paris on the night of the 23/24 September. I write a few last words in the plane (very 'intimate diary'). Persistent fatigue. Need time to recuperate. Lost four kilos or more in a month (not a bad thing).

Head whirling. Millions of images, sounds, smells. Impossible to put them into any sort of order. In any case, what would be the point?

What is a foreigner? A country, a land, ceases

to be foreign the moment one puts one's foot on it. And the air one breathes immediately becomes one's own.

Strange, in the plane, to find once again French newspapers, the French language. I am sleepy.

I feel as if this five-week journey began a very long time ago. We metamorphose time, sometimes. I know that in Paris my wife and my friends will be astonished to see us return so soon. We will ask what had been happening in France. Oh, not much, they will reply. As usual. Yet we ourselves are coming back from across several centuries.

India is not necessarily a phantom. A place where everything seems to have been foreseen, from one extreme to the other. Anything that one can do with this or with that. Complete. The least boring in the world, that is certain. A meticulous exploration of reality. Continuity of ancient kingdoms, the only one left. A gigantic anomaly: unless all the other countries are shadows of India.

Proof that everything has been anticipated: one day in Bombay, in the business area, I stop in front of a tree. A rope has been tied around a branch and hangs down along the trunk. The end of the rope is burning slowly.

I am a little surprised at this unknown ritual, in

the middle of the city. All the more because nobody seems to be looking after it.

And then a man arrives, stops, takes a cigarette out of his pocket and lights it with the end of the dangling, smouldering rope.

It is, in fact, a public lighter.

Who said, Civilisation?

I often think of Hippolyte Fauche, this obscure nineteenth-century Sanskritist who gave us the almost complete French version of the poem (the only one in the world, apart from the Indian languages, and English. But the first English translation, before Lal's, was done by Indians in Bombay around 1900, which is to say, after the French).

This man worked through subscriptions. Initially, he had two or three hundred clients who died one by one over the years. Towards the end a few dozen of them were left. Fauche worked everywhere—even under a bridge, at night, during a storm. I can imagine his regret when he knew he was dying without having completed it. For me he has become a hero, on par with those whose exploits he translated.

In Paris in 1983, we meet again Professor Lal from Calcutta who is continuing with his huge translation in verse. He is giving a lecture at the Kwok On museum and Jacques Pimpaneau asks me to come and translate. With pleasure. In the audience of a few hundred people, arrive suddenly Joyce Mansour (the French-Egyptian poet) and Henri Michaux (also a poet, and a writer and painter), whom I don't know. They sit down in the front row.

Lal has chosen to comment on two lesser-known stories from the *Mahabharata* which are not directly linked to the main flow of the narrative. I translate as best I can, under Michaux's brilliant gaze, so close to me. One of the stories is about a master and his young disciple who sit down one day under the shade of a tree. The master asks the disciple—a very young man—to go and get him some water to drink. The young man goes to a village, meets a beautiful young woman near a well, falls in love with her, follows her home, asks her parents for her hand, marries her, lives there with her, brings up several children, lives out his life. When his hair has turned grey he suddenly remembers his master, takes up a pot of water, goes running back to the tree. There he finds his master who says to him: 'I was waiting.'

The flexibility, the inconsistency of time. A story, a game. With resonances.

At the end, after many exchanges and comments, Michaux came to me and said smilingly, that I had translated 'with the casualness of a naughty boy'. He did not seem disapproving.

Up to what point can this casualness be pushed? Two dangers always threaten every adaptation: a systematic lack of respect which treats the original work like a springboard to who knows not what interpretation and which disfigures and transforms everything—or absolute respect which holds the original as sacrosanct, to the minutest detail.

Somewhere between the two. Yes, but easy to say.

I start to write. Nine years earlier, from 1974, after listening to Lavastine's stories, I tried to write a play. Just to see. Depending heavily on a narrator. Obviously, everything has to start afresh.

The auditions also begin. Because a date has been fixed for the first performances: Avignon, in July 1985. Before that we will do some performances at the Bouffes. This meant starting rehearsals around August or September 1984. Just as well if the play were written before that.

Peter quite frequently asked me to take part in the auditions, talk with the actors, who had come sometimes from the other ends of the world. The scene would often be just written, which meant a double audition—for the actor as much as for the scene. For me it meant seeing whether it worked, whether something stirred, came to life.

All that one discovers—the weaknesses above all—while acting.

The Search Continues
1984

DELHI
MYSTERIOUS
OCCUPATION

Second trip. Departure 31 March. Work well advanced in the past eighteen months. A tryout for one week in November 1982, at the Bouffes theatre, with actors, musicians (particularly the violinist Subramaniam from Madras). Looking for a common factor, archaic sounds, rhythms—also words. And other long sessions of work during the whole of 1983 (among other writings and travels). And the auditions which carried on. Casting very difficult: sixteen principal roles.

It was time to return to India. A felt need.

Delhi, first of all, for just one night.

What were we looking for? As usual, we had no idea.

This time Chloé Obolensky came with us (she was to do the sets, the costumes); so did Kim Menzel, the Danish musician whom we were to meet in Madras where he was finally able to extract some sounds (after a month of trying) from Indian wind instruments.

We drive down towards the south, from Bangalore towards Mysore.

Still looking out for atmosphere, images, sounds, gestures, perfumes, colour.

Stopping every thirty kilometres, or twenty. Always wanting to stop, always looking for an excuse to stop.

Life along the way: grains spread out to dry, vegetables just asking to be squashed by passing cars, animals roaming around, countless pedestrians, birds chased away.

Driving at around thirty kilometres an hour. Surprises all the time.

Extravagant hotel near Mysore, on the top of a hill full of monkeys. The former palace of a maharaja. Each room is different, with amazing furniture of the 1920s. We are the only clients which means that we can each have two rooms—and go from one to the other in the middle of the night. Can't sleep (the heat, a little fever). Dozens of servants dressed in white in a colossal, red-draped dining room.

Just below the hotel, a noisy temple, full of life, fairly primitive. Throngs of women pressed together, screaming. It is said to be a gypsy temple. As sometimes happens, Peter is not allowed to enter, except into the courtyard, because of his light-coloured hair and blue eyes. Since I have very short hair and a bronzed skin, they let me in. I sometimes pretend I am from Kashmir, even pronouncing a few words in some strange lingo. Usually it works. One time I picked up a young child (they are everywhere) and entered into the sanctum sanctorum carrying the child in my arms. No one said anything to me.

Coming out of the temple I put him back where I had found him.

I have started to write, without haste. I try to find the tone, the vocabulary. I make lists of words strictly forbidden to me, all those which carry in them something Occidental, parasitical (no word is neutral or innocent). Such as the word 'noble', the word 'knight', which is connected with our folklore, our history. Impossible to use 'javelin' (inseparable, for some, from images of the Roman legionaries). Even 'lance' or 'sword' are suspect, 'sabre' is banished. A horse cannot be a 'mount' because it seems that the cavalry did not exist. 'Unseat' is unsuitable, 'prophet' too Biblical. Every little phrase poses a problem. Certain concepts such as that of 'dharma' are impossible to translate. It has to be explained (as it is in the heart of the book), undoubtedly by inventing a scene. Vyasa, the legendary author of the poem, says that the aim of the *Mahabharata* is 'to inscribe the dharma in the heart of man'. No question of leaving that out. It is a complex notion that everyone talks about. There is an individual dharma which each one must know and follow, and also a collective, universal, cosmic dharma which one could call the world order. And one depends on the other. If a great number of people respect their individual dharmas, the cosmic dharma will be maintained. That is where our responsibility (and it is a great responsibility) lies, that on which depends the survival of the universe.

According to Lavastine, this sense of menace, of an imminent rupture, of a tragic rejection of dharma, is the centre of the work. This is why the grass is afraid during the battle. Fearful that the dharma might be forgotten by the fault of men, by their arrogance and greed. Impossible to leave this out. That would be a real betrayal. Lavastine says that for him the most important sentence of the book is: 'The dharma, when it is protected, protects. When it is destroyed, it destroys.'

Certain scenes are a must. They cannot be avoided. For example, the scene where Kunti reveals to Karna that he is her son, her illegitimate and rejected son, and that the Pandavas against whom he was making war, were his brothers. Perhaps the positioning of the scene needed to be changed, brought in earlier (than in the poem), into the first days of the battle. But I already have enough elements to start writing. Start with that, maybe. Then go back to the beginning, as in a patchwork. The possibilities—and the task—seem unlimited. The months pass, more travels, a play to be done—and I still don't have the courage to write.

In other, more obvious, cases, one can invent scenes which do not exist in the poem. Introduce characters, imagine relationships, new situations. Indispensable: when Karna receives the ultimate weapon from the hands of the hermit Parasurama (himself an avatar of Vishnu)—another ineluctable scene—in the poem all that is said is: 'He gave him a weapon.' A way must be found of visualising this redoubtable gift. Invent today, if not Indian myths, at least some mythological details unknown or ignored up to now.

A few words, generally monosyllabic, traverse centuries and cultures without being affected. Words which have a certain radiance, a certain resonance, which are open to several meanings, like *blood, heart, flesh, life, breath.*

A Sanskrit expression which we today call (without any sexual connotation) the subconsoncious speaks of 'the secrets movements of the atman'. How can that be translated? I struggled a long time with it. Then I found in the works of Amadou Hampáté-Bâ, specifically in *L'etrange destin de Wangrin* (The Fortunes of Wangrin) the expression 'the depth of your being'. I jumped on it immediately. It seemed very well suited to the characters in the poem. As when Krishna, seemingly suspicious of the moral integrity of Bhishma when he decides to take part (despite his reluctance) in the war, says to him,

'Are you sure in the depth of your being, that it is not your supremacy which you want to demonstrate?[5]

In Madras, to Peter, Kim, Toshi and Marie-Hélène, I read out a possible beginning. About twenty minutes. Just to gauge their reactions—which were not bad. But it is not quite there yet. The beginning is decisive and unquestionably there must be a child (as in the poem, which is recited to an adolescent).

I imagined a temple with people lying down, apparently asleep. A child enters, looks around him. One of the people (it is Vyasa) speaks to him in the shade, 'Do you know how to write?'

This sentence should be the very first one. It prepares the arrival of Ganesha, the celestial scribe sent by Brahma himself. Because Vyasa who had composed it, did not know how to write. He needed someone to do so.

The other actors could get up one by one,

---

5. This sentence would finally be modified but the expression 'the depth of the heart' reappears many times in the narrative. Later I found the same expression being used by Claude Lèvi-Strauss to translate the words of the Amerindians (in *The Jealous Potter*). Had he also read Hampâté-Bâ? Strange, and interesting, triangle.

according to their order of appearance in the story.[6]

I write all over the place, at airports waiting for planes which would not arrive. In a traffic jam in Madras I read out a scene to Peter. The story, the characters, are now constantly with us. It is about time. We start rehearsals in September.

The *Mahabharata* is in a way, a long poem about forgetfulness. Beauty forgotten, the harmony of the earth forgotten, forgotten by man his origins and his place in the scheme of things. They are all born through divine relations and find themselves enmeshed in problems down here. As if the puppet's strings were broken. On many occasions the characters must be asking themselves, 'But what has happened?'

A *reminder*. Imperative to be vigilant. We are responsible for everything, and first of all for ourselves. Must not forget anything (forgetting is easy, alluring). The poem promises to those who read it, good health and a long life. The most potent talisman in the world. Who we are. Vyasa decided to tell us, without flattery. 'You are that' (and nothing else; pointless to look further).

---

6. This beginning would be modified. The first sentence remains, but Vyasa is alone with the child in the wilderness, beside a little lake.

I remember a short passage from Cioran: 'Man is a deceitful animal. History is his punishment.'

Chloé shows us textiles or rather teaches us how to see them, touch them, feel them.

Is there a secret relationship with writing? Fabrics have a woof and a weft, some are tightly knit, others are lighter, heavier, coarser, impalpable; they have their own smell. In the same manner should there be some tightly constructed scenes, some looser, more roughly sketched? The very *stuff* of a scene. A scene made of jute, a scene made of silk.

Two ravishingly beautiful young women—their mother as well—in Madras. Exquisite, of great refinement, slightly haughty, or anyway, distant. They are in the dyeing and block-printing business. One of the daughters—who speaks fluent French—is super-elegant. She takes me to visit her factory where an indistinguishable mass of slaves splashes around in a sort of brown mud. I ask her: 'Is this an old Indian technique?'

'Yes,' she tells me. 'But I attended a three-week workshop in the Ardèche (in the south of France).'

By car up to Cannanore, with a breakdown on the way, in a forest.

As it becomes night, we are taken to a village feast. A long walk along a beaten path, across a wood. Slightly worrying. But a light weaves through the trees. A peasant, warned of our arrival, has come to meet us with a lantern.

He guides us to the village. We hear a distant music.

It is the feast of the patron-hero, present as an effigy, whose exploits are sung this evening. A group of musicians, among them an albino whom we recognise, having met him in 1982. We had called him 'the missionary's son'.

The *Mahabharata* is here also, in this little village. It is everywhere. Tired, we lie down on the ground, on a bed of leaves. A sense of well-being. Children are asleep. I also fall asleep, despite the insistent beat of the drums.

Awakening at dawn.

The next day, meetings at Cannanore. In the evening, the small temple we love so much. Then a Theyyam, for Chloé to see.

In Kerala, towards the end of the 1960s, men started to emigrate to find work in the Emirates across the way. Directly transported from an agricultural, ancestral culture into modern, petrol-driven salaries, they come back in their holidays loaded with transistors, electric mixers and other objects of civilisation. At this sudden contact with electrical appliances, their wives are immediately stricken with a new sort of depression which has in fact been given a name—*the Kerala depression.*

Specialists from all over the world come here, to study this on the spot. After which they write papers and speak about it in seminars.

In the car to Mangalore, then a plane up to Ahmedabad, much further up, in Gujarat.

10 April

Visit the city, an important textile centre. Fabulous textile museum, run by the Sarabhai family who seem to own the whole city. One member of the family, Mrinalini Sarabhai, is a very well-known dancer. She also runs a dance school. Her daughter Mallika who, it seems, speaks French, could be—so they tell us—a possible Draupadi (we had not found anyone for that role). Unfortunately, she is ill. We cannot meet her.

Draupadi, the 'star of women'.

The next morning we have to drive to Rajasthan.

Before leaving the hotel, without knowing why, I suggest that we phone this Mallika. Marie-Hélène calls. Yes, Mallika is feeling better. Her house is, in fact, on the way to the road north. Hardly a detour.

Peter hesitates a little, then he gives in to destiny. In her superb house we find Mallika, pregnant, recovering from hepatitis. Superb (to me) and yes, French-speaking.

We spend some time with her. An Indian Sophia Loren. A strong woman, intelligent, decisive. She listens smiling, to our project.

We stay hardly twenty minutes.[7]

They say that India is 'structured' according to pure and impure. Usual point of view, very probably false, in any case limited. Peter, anyway, pretends that he only loves impure theatre. Pitilessly distrustful of purity, because pity is of necessity impure.

---

7. Without realising it, we had found Draupadi. Mallika Sarabhai would come to Paris two months later (from New York) to read a few scenes for us. Entering the Bouffes theatre, she bent down to touch the ground. She would stay with us—a precious personal presence as much as the presence of India—throughout the whole adventure. Her son was born just before rehearsals began at the end of August. Because of his birth she arrived a little late in Paris. She acted in French, in English, in the film. Impossible, today, to imagine the *Mahabharata* without her.

Here also things appear less simple than one would expect. In fact, all through the journey or rather our moving around, we hardly notice the separations, the castes. Perhaps because we are ourselves distinct and separate. In the streets one cannot miss seeing the slaves, sweepers, cart-pullers, dark and dried-out, spades in hand, unsmiling, no doubt untouchables. We also see the rich—hidden away, much more idle. But between the two the social texture, in our brief impressions, appears incredibly complicated, often even contradictory.

Who can pretend to understand it clearly? Each time we think we have found the thread, and when we pull on it, it becomes unending; it takes on ramifications, changes colour. The feeling of an inexhaustible world. Of a universe in constant expansion.

It is the dry season. The season of heat and dust.

Along the course of a dried-up riverbed which passes through Ahmedabad, thousands of men and women who come from four hundred kilometres away in the north, to stay for six or seven months. They dig deep trenches, build mud huts and cultivate vegetables which they sell in the city.

From the garden of his sumptuous house, a man dressed in white, part of the Sarabhai family, a glass of fruit juice in his hand, says, pointing to the human ants: 'They make a very good living.'

When the first rains fall from the sky in the month of June, the river flows again, sometimes only for a few hours, and carries away fields, trenches, houses. The migratory peasants leave on foot for their mountains in the north. They will return next year.

A stroll, at night, with Peter. Very hot. Lots of men sleep outside, on beds made of ropes.

One man has set up an open-air cinema. It is a bicycle, or rather a tricycle (the man riding it creates the required electricity by pedalling) which is linked to a sort of coffin-like box with tiny holes pierced in the sides. The 'film' (in fact pieces of ad films stolen from here and there), is projected into the inside of the box. The smallest cinema in the world. The interior is painted like a minuscule theatre with a curtain and even seats. The spectators, not more than five or six at a time, keep standing, looking through the holes. The projectionist pedals. The film (silent) lasts four or five minutes, no more; a hotchpotch of images—karate, a singer who sings without anyone hearing him, some love, some dance. A glimpse of Indian cinema in a few moments.

After the meeting with Mallika, we leave Gujarat for Rajasthan, towards the north. Everything is bone dry. Police checks on the way.

Jodhpur, then Udaipur, then Jaipur. The classic circuit. It is a different country, too Muslim for the *Mahabharata* to have made any special mark. But a very beautiful concert in Jodhpur where an Indian musicologist has brought together some excellent instrumentalists in the open air. Among them a child who plays Indian castanets, his eyes raised to the sky. Evening falls. We are served mango juice and the sound of the kamanche traces designs in the evening air.

Two restful days in the Lake Palace at Udaipur. Everyone tells us that it was here that the James Bond film was shot. But none of us has seen it.

High fever. But I carry on working, and I read some scenes to the others. Reading has become almost a daily ritual.

Here the women wear pants, the men wear robes. Jaipur, the dream of Orientalists. Palaces, hotels, an observatory. And everything is pink.

Half a day in a Rajasthan village. To listen to songs, look at very beautiful costumes and jewellery worn by the women. The inhabitants respect all life, like the Jains. Avoid killing snakes, or swallowing mosquitoes. Very poisonous snakes here.

Noticed the presence of a large number of peacocks in the village. I ask if, by chance, peacocks didn't kill snakes. Oh yes, they reply, it is quite possible.

14 April

Back to Delhi by plane.

One short night at the Imperial and off again the next day to Kathmandu, very early in the morning.

Somebody told us that the Pandavas, in the course of their exile, had retreated to Nepal. So let us go and see if any vestiges remain of that.

No, nothing. A disastrous impression. From Kathmandu to Bhakhtapur (the town restored by the Germans), all the men we meet appear drunk, or drugged. Beaten down, an air of defeat. Among buildings restored are men destroyed. It is a festival day.

Everything depresses us, even the sight of the young virgin-goddess at her window, even the visit to the great Buddhist monastery (where I buy some Bhutanese cloth). Ninety-five per cent of Nepal's resources come from foreign aid.

Everything that can be designed to keep a people down. Never forget forgetfulness.

In the evening a dreary walk through the streets.

Sadness. Not even the heart to rebel. The Indian rupee which is not convertible and which no one outside India seems to want, is much sought after here.

Decide to leave the next day.

A plane for Benaras. Arrival into a furnace. The impression, on leaving the plane, of breathing something hotter than oneself. Immobile in the taxi which takes us to a hotel, we are drenched in sweat. It is 41 degrees in the shade. I think I have never, not even in the Sahara, felt so hot.

Yet, the pleasure of getting back to the vitality of India. You feel it everywhere. That day, a hundred marriages were celebrated in Benaras.

Chloé gets to know Benaras. Flight back to Delhi the next day. A big rat, unmoving, awaits me right in the middle of my room at the Imperial Hotel. I ask him what he is doing there; I explain to him that this is no longer his room, that it is mine, I have the key to it. He turns his back to me and goes tranquilly away, towards the hole in the wall through which he had entered.

In the evening of 18 April, a last reading in the hotel, with discussions as always. Peter, Marie-Hélène, Chloé: the first audience. Some scenes already exist.

In the very beginning, in 1974, when the decision

was first made (late one night after an evening at Lavastine's, on the pavement of Saint-André-des-Arts street), Peter said to me: 'We'll stage it when it is ready. And it will take as long as it takes.' The stories, to us, seemed magnificently mysterious. And unknown, in that marketplace far away.

Bit by bit it became clear that the play would be divided into three parts. The last would be called 'The War'. Naturally. Long and difficult (more than three hours), but it would hold. Plenty of action. Difficult comings and goings from one camp to the other. After which it would be necessary to move rapidly between the war and paradise (the audience would be completely worn out, that much was certain).

The second part would be 'The Exile in the Forest', with the return from the forest, and the embassies, just before the war. With all Krishna's efforts to avoid war, knowing full well that it was inevitable. This is the most varied part and also the most attractive; plenty of parallel stories such as Arjuna confronting Shiva in the Himalayas, the disguises in the court of King Virata, the battle of the cows.

The most difficult: the first part. It would have to include the game of dice, a scene lasting almost one hour. But the rest? The origins, the births, childhood, the tournament, marriage, different fights, Krishna's entrance on the stage—how to make all that hold

together? For the moment it seems impossible, unless one were to simply speed up the rhythm and let everything pass by like a film clip—which would be a real betrayal.

Long discussions. Continued the next day.

What becomes clearer, little by little: the need to find our own path. Tradition here is very strong, with an energy that is constantly renewed. How is it that such ancient heroes, with their stories so well-known (we have seen 'The Death of Abhimanyu' seventeen times!) retain such power, almost primeval, after so many centuries?

We cannot hope for anything to equal it. In the West we will, on the contrary, present an *unknown* story. Therein lies the danger of exoticism, of picturesqueness. We must establish from the start that it interests us directly, that it is written for us, that it is in no way a cultural duty.

On the other hand, in India, this all-powerful and omnipresent tradition must have a paralysing effect on contemporary expression. And even beyond that: to continue a tradition does it not mean, in a way, that the order of things is good as it is, that the caste system is excellent and that nothing must be touched? The first wish of an angry young author today must be to throw everything out, including the theatrical conventions.

I know perfectly well that our problem does not lie there, but all the same. It is at least worth thinking about.

Journey's End—And a Beginning
1985

EVERYWHERE   JCC

On 29 January, after four months of rehearsals, we leave for India with the whole group of actors (without Mallika, who knows the story) and some of our technicians.

Plunge the actors—who already know their roles—into the heat, noise, pulsating energy of India.

Great excitement.

From Paris to Bombay and, without stopping, directly from Bombay on to Mangalore, from Mangalore to Udipi. Difficult to imagine a more radical change.

The whole of the 31st at the Yakshagana school to which we return with pleasure. The next day by bus to Cannanore, to the still crumbling Seaside Hotel. In the evening, Theyyam. The next day Kalamandalam, lunch at a temple in Calicut, off banana leaves on the floor. Then, after the Kathakali, to Trichur. Reunion with known roads, familiar smells. But this time very rapidly.

In the evening, we are allowed in to the Koodiyattam (or Kutiyattam) centre; a different school, the oldest and to some the most authentic, the best preserved.

It is late evening. A big dilapidated building. It is very dark, as everywhere in India when night descends. We had learnt of the existence of a very great guru, old and tired. We are permitted to see him for a minute.

We enter a room and sit on the floor. Ten minutes later, literally, they bring him to us. He can no longer walk. Heavy, fat, very old. A simple white lungi. His assistants set him down (with a hundred marks of respect) into an armchair opposite us. A man who has danced his whole life long. Someone explains to him who we are and what we are looking for in India. He keeps his eyes shut, he listens, breathes fast. We can hear his difficult breathing.

Then he says something in a low voice. They translate for us: the master will offer you a sample of his art. He will show us 'the young girl who goes to her first rendezvous with love.'

And he actually shows us. His eyelids lift open, his eyes become animated, he blinks, the hint of a smile plays on his lips, he raises one of his hands, sketches a gesture.

For a few minutes, he is no longer himself. This very old man, at death's door, becomes a young girl, ardent and expectant. He shows us, and how; with no props, nothing.

Then, suddenly, it is all over. And they carry him away.

❖

3 February

Very early departure by bus for Madurai. First elephant on the way: everyone rushing to the door, photos, etc.

Twenty kilometres before Palani, we start overtaking people walking down the road carrying strange, light wooden structures more or less in the form of houses.

Quite accidentally we have chanced upon the day of a great pilgrimage. An immense crowd at Palani. We stop. It lasts more than three hours. Millions of pilgrims are conducted through streets cordoned off with ropes held by students.

The temple is on the top of a high, rocky hill. One goes up on a big cableway, or on foot for the more energetic ones. At the top, visitors are led into the sanctuary by vociferous and agitated Brahmins. Absolutely nothing sacred about it. Naturally, it is a Shiva temple.

We descend on foot, some down the hillside, others by the steps. Almost at every step, holding out his bowl, a monster. Some of them are quite extraordinary. One might well believe that all the sick beggars of India have come together here. Long garland of what humanity could be, could have been. Their looks, as we pass by.

Their hands held out. The absence of hands.

And from place to place, in their midst, a very beautiful child-god, made-up and indifferent.

Sixteen different nationalities, in our group. Cohesion of colours. Mirror, my beautiful mirror. How well one feels with others. Like a little world within the world, doing at his level what the whole wide world does not. There is here (and vice versa?).

The play is written, naturally, since we have been rehearsing it for four months. But anything is still possible.

It has been a stupendous job (everyone admits that), but Peter knows how to give the impression, to me, to the actors, that he works without actually working. It is a path always full of surprises. We learn martial arts, shoot with bows and arrows, travel around India, watch performances; and the work gets done through all that. As if the moments of solitude indispensable for a writer (moments which last many hours) were also a part of this pleasure.

Without speaking of the invisible work, the most precious of all.

Return to Madurai (3 February) and to the great temple. Vittorio (Mezzogiorno) stops for a moment near some women selling objects spread out on the ground. He knows he is to play Arjuna, he is preparing for that. During a year of exile, Arjuna, the great warrior, in order not to be recognised, chose to disguise himself as a woman and become a dance teacher to a king's daughters.

There, at the entrance to the temple, he picks some ankle bells and has them tied to his ankles. He even tries them out. Great astonishment all around at this blue-eyed European who beats the ground with his bare feet.

Arriving from Italy, Vittorio came to see me one day in Paris, at the very beginning of the rehearsals (another actor had dropped out of playing the role). Not knowing anything about the poem, he asked me to tell him about it. Both of us in the kitchen. After five or six minutes he interrupted me to say: 'If I understand correctly, what you are asking me is much more than acting.'[8]

In the evening, as it happened, a big festival. The

---

8. It was much more, and he felt it. For him it became a total involvement. Quite magnificent. He acted in the play and in the film, in both versions. Five years altogether. Everyone loved him. Cancer carried him off despite his courage, in 1994. The third one of the group to leave, after Duta Seck and Ryszard Cieslak.

day when the great idols (three tall, golden statues, one of them a horse) are taken out of the temple and carried to the lake. A colossal crowd. A million strong. We quickly get separated. I literally allow myself to be carried off by the crowd which presses tightly against me, though without any problem. Quite the opposite. I go where the crowd goes, I don't take any initiative, I do nothing, I follow the movement. Almost intoxicating.

After going around the lake, the splendid idols are taken back to the temple until the next year. The crowd parts. Some of us find ourselves in front of the main entrance and we reassemble to enter together. They allow us to go up to the sanctum sanctorum, a room carpeted with sculpted golden plaques. It is late, past midnight. Barely a few dozen of the faithful. We copy them. We pass the palms of both hands across the bowl of flames which is presented before us and press them, still warm, against our faces. The last ritual before getting to the hotel. We will go to bed purified.

We all leave Madurai on 5 February for a morning in the forest. Still the same quest: see, feel, listen, to an Indian forest. Many scenes during the exile of the Pandavas, take place in a forest, the place of exile and apparently of solitude.

Visit to a small temple on a mountain. Full of life. Meet a child-god, made-up, decked out in peacock feathers. He suddenly appears in front of us, at a bend in the forest trail. Not a word. Face calm, a distant look in his eyes. All he wants is a rupee or two. Young divinity who begs in the forest.

In the middle of the forest we find a small temple in ruins. A platform, six by four metres, is surrounded by a sort of terrace where one can sit.

A brief pause. Peter asks each one of us to go into the forest for twenty or so minutes, and bring back an object that we find particularly striking.

No sooner said than done. We go and we come back, with a pebble, a leaf, a branch, a handful of earth, a long palm frond, a dead insect.

We pile up all these objects in the middle of our terrace. And we start our daily exercises: first the vocal then the physical. We must present a strange spectacle: twenty-five people, Europeans, Africans, a Japanese, a Balinese, most of them in odd costumes, singing at the top of our voices in the thick of the forest, signalling, gesticulating, improvising, reading out pieces of the text.

No Indian forest is completely deserted. Peasants, woodcutters pass us by, looking at our group with curiosity, with astonishment. And there is something to be astonished about, even in India.

All of a sudden a woman, a peasant, approaches.

Without any hesitation, she walks the few steps up to our terrace and, without casting a glance at us, lies down flat on the ground with both arms outstretched, hands folded, towards the heap of objects we have collected from the forest.

She has seen what looks like an offering; she has come spontaneously to pay homage to it.

We watch in silence, holding our breath.

Simplicity, omnipresence of fervour. Like a very special welcome.

She stays about a minute, stretched out on the ground. Then gets up, leaves the group (still without a word being spoken) and goes off into the forest.

We remain silent a long time. That day we do not go back to our exercises.

The African actors who are part of the journey, four of them, are Tamsir Niane, called Fifi: witty and lively; the great Sotigui Kouyaté who is getting on for fifty and will play the impeccable Bhishma; the strong Mamadou Dioume who will be Bhima, and the odd Clement Masdongar, originally from Chad, a trained dancer, handsome, brilliant, endearing and slightly unstable.

They all find themselves in India for the first time and their reactions are similar: everything reminds them of Africa. They keep saying: this is like at home, it is like in Africa. Direct and profound links, even with the landscapes. But most of all in the way of thinking, the rituals, the rhythms.

One evening, having got a splinter in my foot, I knock at Sotigui's door as his room is next to mine. I ask him to take out the splinter. He takes my foot between his hands and first of all murmurs something in Bambara.

Then he puts on his glasses, takes a needle and removes the splinter.

From Madurai to Madras by plane. On 6 February, the whole day in Kanchipuram.

We find Shankaracharya, this time in a sanctuary in Kanchipuram, a vast maze, rather strange, in the centre of the sacred city (the Benaras of the South). The rooms are like a labyrinth full of scribes, visitors, devotees carrying offerings, well-dressed men walking by briskly in animated discussion. Papers, odours.

Four servants (slaves?) struggle to push a big elephant through a doorway. It had strayed in there and now could not get out. That is certainly going to take time.

Our group is received first of all by the person we had met three years earlier; the middle-aged Shankar. Long and interesting conversations with the actors.

Each of them wants to learn something special about his character. Here too, we are on a terrace.

I have to submit to a sort of test. The Brahmins place before me a large parcel of paintings, of ex-votos, all representing mythological scenes. As I am a 'writer', the Ganesha, the one who dares to write the story of the poem, I ought to know these scenes, be able to say who is who. They show them to me one by one. I don't do too badly (not an easy test because the bearded men all look alike in the paintings, and all the women are the same).

After this we are admitted into the presence of the saint himself, the very famous, very old Shankaracharya, who has not opened his mouth for close to eight years.

We are led into a small courtyard. They ask us to sit on the ground, which we do. It is morning. We wait in silence for a good hour, facing a small, closed door. A modest building, worn-out. Peeling walls. A few hens moving around us; a little further away, the crows.

Nothing solemn, nothing special. Sainthood suffices. Quite something.

Finally the door opens. A very old man, wearing a lungi, appears. A closed face, almost severe. A squint in one eye.

He stops in the doorway and barely glances at us. He seems to be in a bad mood (disturbed?). He nods his head, first to the left then to the right. A Brahmin comes running and, without a word, brings him the day's newspaper.

The old saint—one of the most revered men in the world who is known to have performed miracles—stays a long while on the doorstep, looking a little sullen—or distracted. He looks without looking, newspaper in hand. To the right, then to the left. This lasts six or seven minutes. We don't stir.

Finally, he makes a sign with his hand (a benediction? For us?), goes back inside and closes the door behind him.

It is over.

We leave in silence.

A little later Maurice Bénichou (preparing to be the first Western actor to play Krishna) does us an excellent imitation of the old saint.[9]

---

9. We saw him four years later, during a series of theatre workshops which we conducted in India in 1989. He was nothing more than a very old man, lying on the ground. The crowd pressed together in front of a curtain. Then the Brahmins pulled the curtain and we could see him, curled up on the floor, wearing a pair of large spectacles, very emaciated. He no longer moved at all. They showed him for an instant, still alive, and then let the curtain fall again.

Big Bhishma in Madras

After this we are received by the young Shankaracharya whom I have now known for several years but without ever having heard him speak.

He seems more dry, more reserved, more stern, more 'fundamentalist' than the middle-aged man. But as soon as he starts to speak he comes alive, even smiles. He shows a profound knowledge of the work, the *Gita* especially, and has some personal interpretations. The idea of a performance in the West, in France, is surprising to him but he accepts it ('the *Mahabharata* is good for you', a sentence we heard often). He tries to imagine how such a performance could be possible, outside Indian traditions and technique. Peter tells him that is precisely our problem.

What part, ultimately, should India play in our work? The manner of telling, the *mise en scéne*, the manner of acting, the costumes, the music: all pose problems. Quite obviously we cannot offer an Indian presentation. We are incapable of it. It would be ridiculous, absurd. Nor could we appropriate the poem, transport it to the West in our own style, ignoring on the way its culture of origin. Impossible, certainly, to write it in the form of a *tragedy*, of a *dramatic* work. I accepted that a long time ago. A part of the storytelling has to stay. Peter told the actors: 'You have to be storytellers with twenty-five faces.'

Could we, for example, keep the names as

they are? Is it even conceivable to present in Paris, in Avignon, a play where the actors are called Yudhisthira, or Dhrishtadyumna?

Too late to change, in any case.

In Kanchipuram, at the end of the day, they let a sacred elephant out from one of the temples and allow him to roam about freely in the town.

I saw him, one evening, going towards the market street, in the middle of fruit and vegetable sellers. He delicately picked a lettuce here, a banana there, with the tip of his trunk. And nothing was refused to him.[10]

A sentence of Henri Michaux which could be applied to the *Mahabharata*: 'You tell this story to an old stick; it will sprout leaves and take root.'

The plane from Madras to Calcutta.

The day of 7 December in Calcutta. Many meetings with actors and storytellers, who already

---

10. During our trip in 1989, we learnt that the middle-aged Shankaracharya, that kind and smiling man, apparently quite worldly, had suddenly gone into retreat. He had taken refuge in solitude, somewhere in the Himalayas. No further news from him. Another young man has been called upon. He is seventeen. The baton is passed.

knew us. Accompanied, naturally, by the cultural attaché.

In a group, they say, one individual never belongs but remains a loner. This was the case with Georges Corraface. The bus hardly stopped somewhere and he disappeared. When it was time to leave we looked for him. A phrase constantly on Marie-Hélène's lips, 'Where is Georges?'

Night train from Calcutta to Benaras.

A mass of people at the station. The usual apparent disorder so secretly ordered. Sotigui, ill, vomits on the platform.

The windows of the trains are barred. We are told that thieves at night, at the stations, do not hesitate to cut off the hands of the sleeping travellers to steal their rings and watches.

Peter and I are in a sleeper with two others, one Muslim, the other Sikh. They get up several times, each in his turn, to perform their devotions.

I don't get a wink of sleep. But that is how it is: one sleeps very little in India, at least in our case.

Benaras at dawn. Peter, Marie-Hélène and I—and also Maurice Bénichou who came once in between—can now become guides for others. We recognise places, sometimes even shortcuts, shops.

All of us on a big boat. Slowly, in silence. Towards

evening, as we move towards the cremation fires, Kudsi, our Turkish musician, takes up his flute and plays a little. *Apropos*, he has to find out what Krishna played on his flute. Not easy.

Meditation in front of the pyres. One gets the impression that that's all there is to it. A burnt leg and a foot stick out. One of the men in charge breaks the leg with one blow and pushes it back into the fire.

After this, I get lost in the small streets of the town, along with Maurice (Bénichou). Everything reminds him of the *souks* of his childhood in North Africa. We pass in front of a bas-relief where Krishna saves Draupadi from being disrobed at the end of the game of dice by lengthening her sari indefinitely. One of the rare ancient representations of this episode.

Then we really get lost. It takes us good hour to find the others back at the hotel.

Between Marie-Hélène, Peter and me, the *Mahabharata* is like a code. We see someone: it is a Shakuni, or a Kunti. The poem constantly comes between us and the world. We also speak of our dharma, which sometimes creates zones of incomprehension. We understand the contemporary political games in the light of Krishna's.

'Krishna' signifies black. And it is true. The work is full of darkness; it accepts it and sometimes demands it.

Everything is dark. We light a candle; it confines itself to a circle of light surrounded by darkness. A second candle: the circle gets enlarged. Ten, a hundred, candles. One sun, ten suns, a million suns: the circle of light is gigantic, it seems infinite. But it is always encircled by the dark arms of Krishna.

'What can cover the earth completely?' the lake asks Yudhisthira. The reply: 'Darkness'.

For the scene where the lake questions Yudhisthira (a true test because the lake is his hidden father), I need other questions than those posed in the poem. I reread Plutarch, especially, in his *Life of Alexander*, the part about the meeting between the young conqueror surrounded by Greek philosophers and the Indian sages come to greet them.

The Greeks ask, the Indians reply. For example, 'What came first, the day or the night?' The Indians reply, 'The day, but it only preceded the night by one day.'

Another question: 'Which is the cleverest animal?' The Indian response: 'The one that man has not yet managed to find.'

I feel like putting some of these question-answers into the play. Have I the right? I phone Georges Dumézil who has become interested in our project.

I ask him if I can mix Plutarch with the *Mahabharata* for some exchanges.

'But of course,' he replies. 'They belong to the same era! And in any case, everything belongs to everybody.'

Last trip to Agra. Inevitable. But this time we won't go to Rajasthan.

Delhi, at last, on 9 December.

It all ends with an open-air feast to which we are invited by Rajeev Sethi, our elegant adviser, our friend from the very beginning. In a beautiful, ruined old fort, outside the city. Dancers, puppeteers, magicians (with, at every turn, the unforgettable words: '*Begui, begui* and … gingerly')! Peter goes on for a long time about the word 'gingerly'.

Half reclining on carpets with cushions, drinks—and a buffet. Very pleasant, without a shadow of doubt.

The *Mahabharata* awaits us in Paris. It is the end of the last holidays. End also of my notes (in the plane on the return journey) and the beginning of anxiety. Each one of us feels it: this obligation to *play*. What has India given us? Impossible to say. A secret dimension that will remain probably always secret, beyond wonder, charm, irritation, repulsion. The pulsating energy, above all else, and the mixture of things. The closeness that one only finds when working together and which no one can define. To travel in order not to see, travel to do, or to be.

The play opens in three months.

AFTERWORD

Naturally, our relationship with India did not end there. I myself have returned frequently in the past ten years, either with Peter or for other reasons. In 1994, I even spent two weeks in Dharamshala in the Himalayas, with the Dalai Lama, and we co-published a book, *Violence and Compassion*. Today I have plans for a film with Mani Kaul, a longtime friend. An Indian film, to be produced by Suresh Jindal and shot in India (in 1998?), an adaptation of an episode in the *Mahabharata* (again!) and entitled *The Dicing*. I have been accepted officially as an Indian scriptwriter, the first non-Indian. I am very proud of it.

One does not separate oneself from the *Mahabharata*. It is a work one gets 'attached' to, one which puts into question all other writing. It is also a new vocabulary, another aspect of our always difficult relations with the world.

An unexplored territory which we carry within ourselves without knowing it. I have often been called upon to speak in public, even in India, on the poem, on the *Gita*, our work, the film that was shown (the play could never be performed in India). I have often written on it, articles and prefaces. I have published, in the form of a narrative, a *Mahabharata* which has been translated into fifteen or so languages. And so on. It will never leave me. And nor have I any desire for a separation, a divorce. 'The *Mahabharata* is good for you.'

Sometimes everything turns upside down. As much as India helped me to write the *Mahabharata* in the form of a play, so now it helps me to live in India, to feel at home there. A poem and a continent; two continents, in fact. Reunited with a place that is multiple, yet one. As Krishna said to Vyasa, the god to the man: 'Which one of us invented the other?'

ALSO FROM SPEAKING TIGER

MAHARISHI AND ME
SEEKING ENLIGHTENMENT WITH THE BEATLES GURU
Susan Shumsky

'Full of fascinating information about TM, its founder Maharishi Mahesh Yogi, and the celebrities who followed him, Susan Shumsky's book *Maharishi & Me* is a captivating read.'—John Gray, bestselling author, *Men Are from Mars, Women Are from Venus*

The year 2018 marks the fortieth anniversary of the Beatles' trip to Rishikesh, to stay at the ashram of their guru, Maharishi Mahesh Yogi. Along with John Lennon, Paul McCartney, George Harrison and Ringo Starr came a host of other celebrities, including pop stars Donovan and Mike Love (of the Beach Boys fame) and actor Mia Farrow.

Amongst them was Susan Shumsky, one of the Maharishi's earliest disciples. In this memoir, she offers an honest and dynamic exposé about a phenomenal, influential spiritual master and the dysfunctional organization he founded. From her ringside view, she tells the story of what really happened at Rishikesh, encounters with many of the Maharishi's famous disciples and her own personal journey from hippiedom to meditation under the tutelage of the man who introduced TM—Transcendental Meditation—to the West.

Page Extent: 340 pp + 16-pp photo insert　　　　　Price: ₹599

ALSO FROM SPEAKING TIGER

TRAVELS ON MY ELEPHANT
AN INDIAN JOURNEY

Mark Shand

'I enjoyed this book immensely. Shand is the most engaging adventurer I have come across.'—Imran Khan

When Mark Shand, an aristocratic playboy and travel writer, decided that what he needed was an elephant, it wasn't long before he started getting phone calls from India, offering elephants for sale. With the help of a Maratha nobleman, he purchased Tara, a young, scrawny female, and travelled with her—and a retinue of friends, old and new—for more than 800 kilometres across India, from Konark to the Sonepur Mela—the world's oldest elephant market.

From Bhim, a drink-racked mahout, he learnt the skills of elephant driving. From his friend Aditya Patankar, he learnt about the culture and attitudes of India. And with Tara, his new companion, he fell in love. So much so, that decades after their travelling days were over, Mark Shand was still fund-raising and campaigning on behalf of Indian elephants, becoming one of the most high-profile conservationists in the world.

Travels On My Elephant is the story of an epic journey across the dusty back roads of India, as Mark Shand and his party astound, amuse and puzzle all those they encounter on the way. It is also a vivid portrayal of a cheerfully chaotic India and the memorable, touching account of Tara's transformation from a sad beggar to the star attraction, and Mark Shand's loyal companion.

Page Extent: 208 pp   Price: ₹299

www.ingramcontent.com/pod-product-compliance
Lightning Source LLC
Chambersburg PA
CBHW051119230426
43667CB00014B/2646